JOHN LEWIS

CONGRESSMAN AND CIVIL RIGHTS HERO

by Rachel Rose

Consultant: Jerald Podair, Professor of History and American Studies, Lawrence University, Appleton, Wisconsin

BEARPORT
PUBLISHING

Minneapolis, Minnesota

Credits

Cover and title page, © Kathy Hutchins/Shutterstock; 4, © Bettmann Archive/Getty Images; 5, © Black Star/Newscom; 6, © Hulton Archive/Getty Images; 7, © Charles Shaw/Getty Images; 8, © Kypros/Getty Images; 9, © /Getty Images; 10, © /Getty Images; 11, © Francis Miller/The LIFE Picture Collection/Getty Images; 12, © Universal History Archive/Getty Images; 14, © /Getty Images; 15, © Bettman/Getty Images; 16, © /Getty Images; 17, © Bettman/Getty Images; 18, © Bill O'Leary/The Washington Post/Getty Images; 19, © Drew Angerer/Getty Images; 20, © Larry French/Getty Images; 21, © Tom Williams/CQ Roll Call/Getty Images; 22, © Universal History Archive/Getty Images; 22, © Bill O'Leary/The Washington Post/Getty Images

President: Jen Jenson
Director of Product Development: Spencer Brinker
Editor: Allison Juda
Photo Research: Book Buddy Media

Library of Congress Cataloging-in-Publication Data

Names: Rose, Rachel, 1968- author.
Title: John Lewis : congressman and civil rights hero / by Rachel Rose.
Other titles: Congressman and civil rights hero
Description: Minneapolis, Minnesota : Bearport Publishing Company, [2021] |
  Series: Bearport biographies | Includes bibliographical references and
  index.
Identifiers: LCCN 2020039245 (print) | LCCN 2020039246 (ebook) | ISBN
  9781647477202 (library binding) | ISBN 9781647477288 (paperback) | ISBN
  9781647477363 (ebook)
Subjects: LCSH: Lewis, John, 1940-2020--Juvenile literature. | African
  American civil rights workers--Biography--Juvenile literature. | Civil
  rights workers--United States--Biography--Juvenile literature. | United
  States. Congress. House--Biography--Juvenile literature. | African
  American legislators--United States--Biography--Juvenile literature. |
  Legislators--United States--Biography--Juvenile literature. | African
  Americans--Civil rights--History--20th century--Juvenile literature.
Classification: LCC E840.8.L43 R67 2021 (print) | LCC E840.8.L43 (ebook)
  | DDC 328.73/092 [B]--dc23
LC record available at https://lccn.loc.gov/2020039245
LC ebook record available at https://lccn.loc.gov/2020039246

For more information, write to Bearport Publishing, 5357 Penn Avenue South, Minneapolis, MN 55419. Printed in the United States of America.

Contents

A Call for Change

More than 250,000 people swarmed the nation's capital for the August 28, 1963, March on Washington. They were there to **protest** the **discrimination** against black Americans. John Lewis stepped up to face the crowd and began to speak. He called for change—for fair treatment and safety for all. He was only 23 years old, but he was ready for the fight.

John spoke to the crowd.

John was the youngest of the six leaders who helped organize the march. They were known as the Big Six.

Marchers packed the National Mall to demand change.

Young Activist

John Robert Lewis was born on February 21, 1940, in Troy, Alabama. His parents were sharecroppers, which meant they farmed land owned by someone else. While John was growing up, there were terrible laws in the southern United States. These laws unfairly **segregated** black people and white people in public places. John knew these laws had to change.

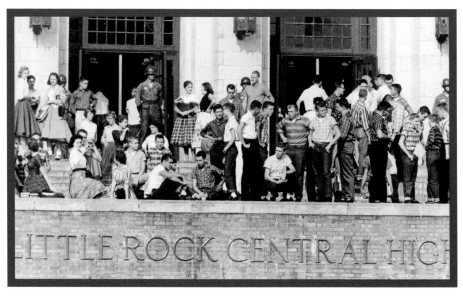

John grew up with segregation, including in schools

John *(left)* with Martin Luther King Jr. *(center)*

As a teenager, John met Martin Luther King Jr. and Rosa Parks. They **inspired** him to speak out against segregation.

By the time John went to college, he was active in the **civil rights movement**. He and other students would go to restaurants that wouldn't serve black people, sit down, and refuse to leave. This type of protest was called a sit-in. John also took part in Freedom Rides, where black and white people rode buses together to challenge segregation.

John was arrested more than 40 times while standing up for equal rights.

John and his fellow protesters were often attacked and arrested by people who did not want segregation to end.

In 1963, John became the **chairman** of the Student Nonviolent Coordinating Committee (SNCC). He would be leading students in civil rights activities. Later that year, he helped organize the March on Washington, where he spoke with **passion** about the need for equal rights for all people. He told the crowd, "We do not want our freedom gradually. We want our freedom now."

Martin Luther King Jr. gave his famous speech at the March on Washington, too.

John *(back row, third from left)* and the other March on Washington leaders

Bloody Sunday

The March on Washington created enough support to pass the Civil Rights Act of 1964. This law made segregation illegal, banned discrimination, and protected the rights of black workers. Despite the law banning discrimination, some Southern states still made it hard for black people to vote. So, on March 7, 1965, John helped lead a peaceful march to bring attention to this issue.

Marchers make their way across Alabama

Over 600 people gathered in Selma, Alabama, to make the 54-mile (87 km) march to Montgomery, Alabama.

As the peaceful marchers crossed the Edmund Pettus Bridge in Selma, they were blocked by police. Soon, officers began pushing marchers down and hitting them with sticks. The attacks were shown on television, and people all over America were very angry. The **violent** day became known as Bloody Sunday and was a turning point in the civil rights movement.

John (*on the ground, left*) and fellow marchers were attacked in Selma.

Eight days after Bloody Sunday, the Voting Rights Act outlawed anything that stopped black people from voting.

The marchers saw police blocking their way as they crossed the bridge, but they bravely went on.

Activist in the House

John left the SNCC in 1966, but he continued to be a key player in the civil rights movement. During the 1970s, he helped register millions of **minority** voters. Then, he decided to become a **politician** so he could make a difference from within government. In 1981, he was elected to Atlanta's city council. In 1987, he joined Congress.

John celebrated after winning the election for Congress.

John would serve in the U.S. House of Representatives for over 30 years.

John pushed for the right to vote. Then, he encouraged everybody to exercise that right.

In Congress, John kept fighting for civil rights and the rights of all people. He was an early champion for the **LGBTQ+** community, helping to push for laws giving its members equality. He also fought for the rights of **immigrants**. In 2013, he was even arrested at a **rally** supporting immigrants.

In 2011, John received the Presidential Medal of Freedom. It was given to him by President Barack Obama.

John knew being arrested was a small price to pay for the rights of immigrants.

Hero until the End

In 2016, John proved his sit-in days were not over. He led a protest on the floor of the House of Representatives to push for changes in gun laws. He continued to speak out until his death on July 17, 2020. From his early years to the end of his life, John stayed true to his goal of fighting for freedom and safety for everyone.

In 2016, John won an award for writing a graphic novel, *March*, that taught young readers about the civil rights movement.

John during his Congress sit-in

Timeline

Here are some key dates in John Lewis's life.

1940
Born on
February 21

1961
Joins the
Freedom Rides

1963
March on
Washington

1964
Civil Rights
Act passes

1965
Helps lead
Selma-
Montgomery
march

1987
Becomes a member
of Congress

2011
Receives the
Presidential Medal
of Freedom

2020
Passes away on
July 17

Glossary

chairman the person who is in charge of a group

civil rights movement the fight for racial equality led by African Americans that began in the 1950s

discrimination the unfair treatment of people because of their race or background

immigrants people who come from one country to live and make their homes in a new one

inspired encouraged by others to do things

LGBTQ+ an acronym that stands for lesbian, gay, bisexual, transgender, queer, and more; a diverse range of sexual orientations and gender identities

minority the smaller in number of two or more groups

passion strong feelings

politician a person who is a member of government

protest to demonstrate against something; this type of demonstration is also called a protest

rally an event where a large group of people come together to offer support or help for a cause

segregated when people are separated by groups, especially by race

violent marked by the use of harmful force

Index

Read More

Doeden, Matt. *John Lewis: Courage in Action (Gateway Biographies)*. Minneapolis: Lerner Publications, 2018.

Harris, Duchess, and Tammy Gagne. *John Lewis: Civil Rights Leader and Congressman (Freedom's Promise)*. Minneapolis: Abdo Publishing, 2020.

Learn More Online

1. Go to **www.factsurfer.com**
2. Enter "**John Lewis**" into the search box.
3. Click on the cover of this book to see a list of websites.

About the Author

Rachel Rose is a writer who lives in San Francisco. Her favorite books to write are about people who lead inspiring lives.